Best of
IN RECITAL SOLOS

ABOUT THE SERIES • A NOTE TO THE TEACHER

Best of In Recital® Solos is a series that focuses on fabulous solo repertoire, intended to motivate your students. The fine composers of this series have created musically engaging pieces, and the wide range of styles in this six-book series is sure to please any student! It will help you to plan students' recital repertoire easily. This series can also be used as weekly motivation and fun, as well as for sight-reading! You will find original solos that emphasize different musical and technical issues, giving you the selections to accommodate all of your student's needs. These fabulous solos are from the following series: *In Recital® Throughout the Year, Volumes 1 and 2*; *In Recital® with Jazz, Blues, and Rags*; *In Recital® with Timeless Hymns*; *In Recital® with Classical Themes*; *In Recital® with All Time Favorites*; and *In Recital® with Popular Music*.

Go to inside-back cover for information on downloading free recordings for this book.

THE
F·J·H
MUSIC
COMPANY
INC.

Frank J. Hackinson

Production: Frank J. Hackinson
Production Coordinators: Peggy Gallagher and Philip Groeber
Cover Design: Terpstra Design, San Francisco, CA
Cover Illustrations: Keith Criss, Marcia Donley, and Sophie Library
Engraving: Tempo Music Press, Inc.
Printer: Tempo Music Press, Inc.

ISBN-13: 978-1-61928-101-1

ORGANIZATION OF THE SERIES
BEST OF IN RECITAL® SOLOS

The series is carefully leveled into the following six categories: Early Elementary, Elementary, Late Elementary, Early Intermediate, Intermediate, and Late Intermediate. Each of the works has been selected for its artistic as well as its pedagogical merit.

Book Five — Intermediate, reinforces the following concepts:

- Dotted quarter, triplet and sixteenth note rhythmic patterns; syncopation.

- Numerous changes of tempo, articulations, and moods.

- Hand-over-hand arpeggios, and extended one-hand arpeggios.

- Broken and blocked octaves.

- Rolled chords, and more sophisticated pedaling.

- Left-hand parts increase in intricacy with more involved accompanimental figures.

- Pieces reinforce the following musical terms and symbols: *espressivo, trill, sotto voce, molto agitato, andante con expressione,* and *una corda*; plus basic musical terminology found in books 1-4.

- A mixture of major and minor keys strengthen the student's command of the piano.

FJH2240

TABLE OF CONTENTS

for Aaron Wyatt

Etude in A Minor

Martín Cuéllar

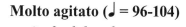

FJH2240

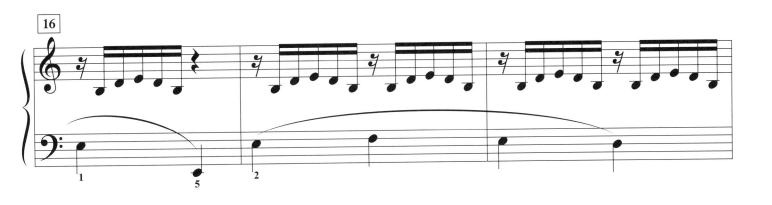

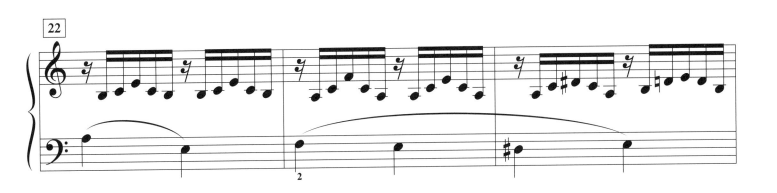

6

Eagle's Flight

Melody Bober

Dance Masquerade

Timothy Brown

FJH2246

As the mask falls

Ragamuffin

Lee Evans

Ragtime feel (♩ = ca. 84) (even ♪'s)

FJH2246

Presto

Valerie Roth Roubos

Molto agitato (♩ = ca. 160)

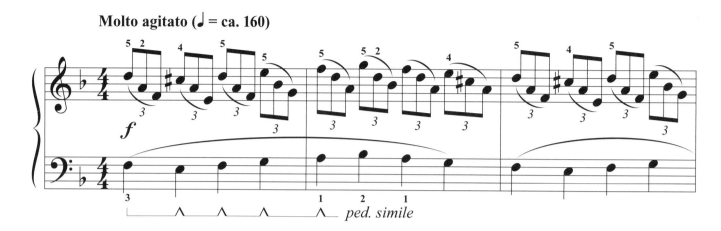

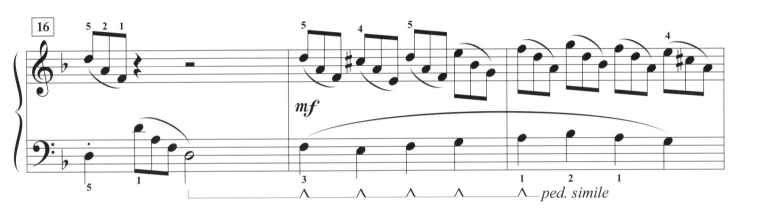

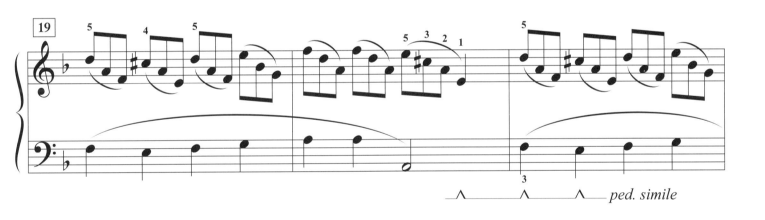

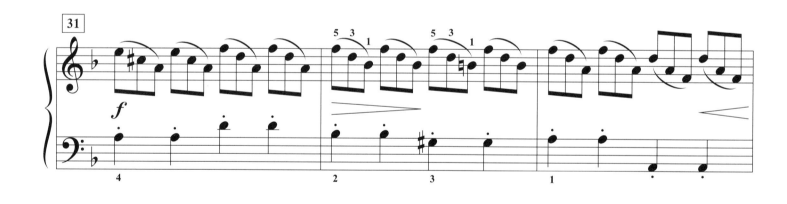

Meditation in the Rain

Timothy Brown

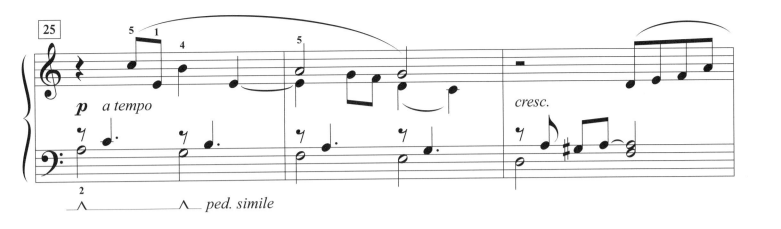

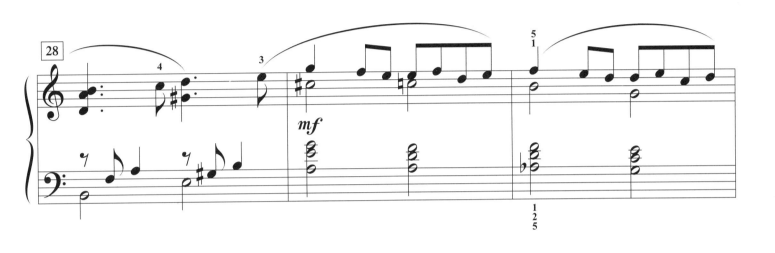

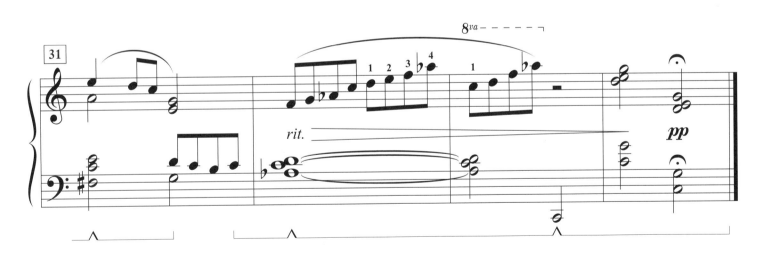

FJH2246

Kickin' It

Edwin McLean

FJH2246

Jazz Toccata

Martín Cuéllar

FJH2240

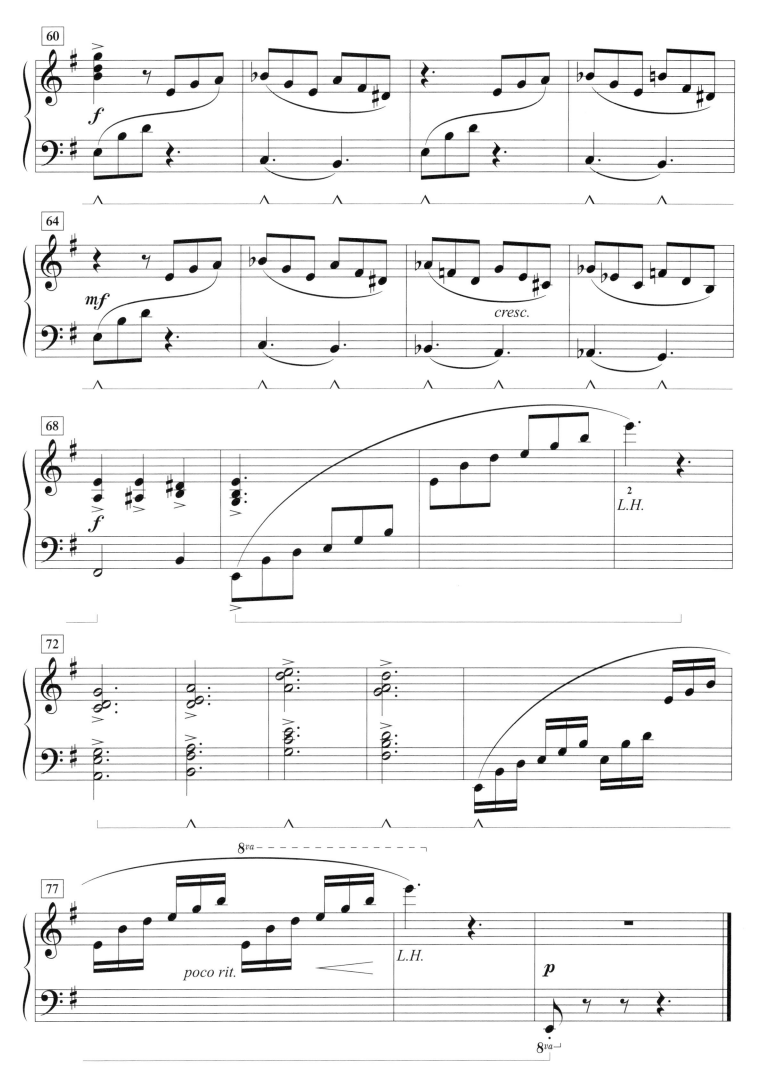

Pavanne

(Opus 50)

Gabriel Fauré
arr. Timothy Brown

Allegretto molto moderato (♩ = ca. 84)

FJH2246

Serenade

Melody Bober

JH2246

Swing Low, Sweet Chariot

African-American Spiritual
arr. Nancy Lau

FJH224

low,   sweet   char -   i - ot,_____

mp

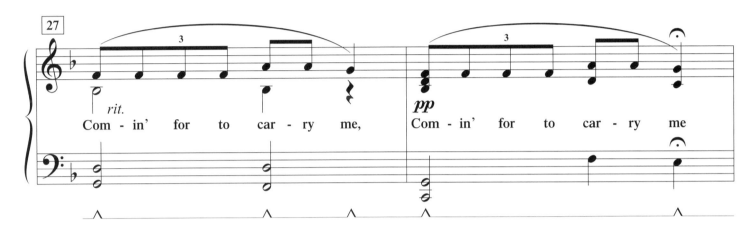

rit.

Com - in'   for   to   car - ry   me,   Com - in'   for   to   car - ry   me

pp

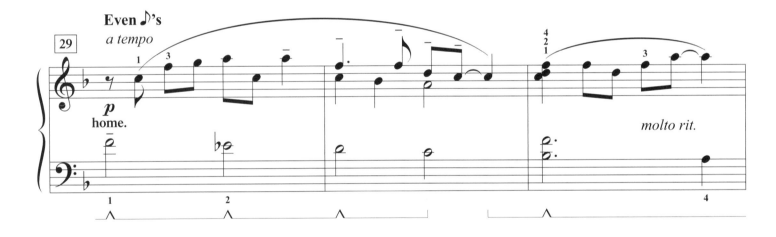

Even ♪'s

a tempo

p

home.

molto rit.

pp

Notturno

Valerie Roth Roubos

FJH2246

FJH2246

Canto de Estío
(Song of Summer)

Martín Cuéllar

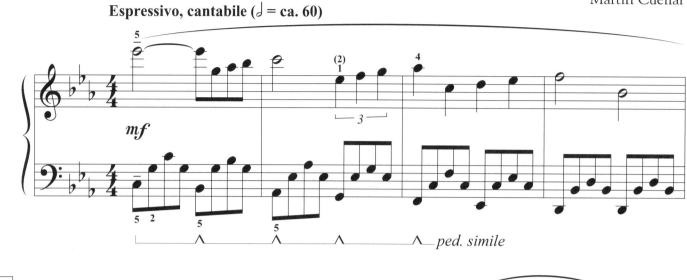

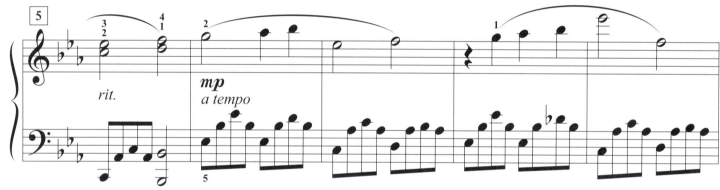

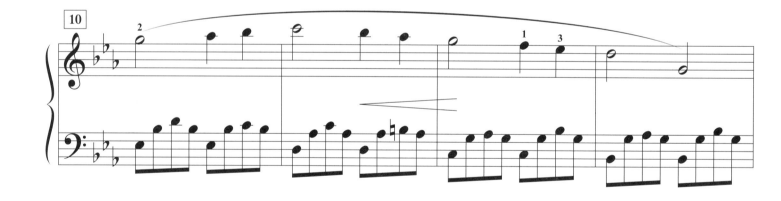

FJH2224

ABOUT THE COMPOSERS AND ARRANGERS

Melody Bober

Piano instructor, music teacher, composer, clinician—Melody Bober has been active in music education for over 25 years. As a composer, her goal is to create exciting and challenging pieces that are strong teaching tools to promote a lifelong love, understanding, and appreciation for music. Pedagogy, ear training, and musical expression are fundamentals of Melody's teaching, as well as fostering composition skills in her students. Melody graduated with highest honors from the University of Illinois with a degree in music education, and later received a master's degree in piano performance. She maintains a large private studio, performs in numerous regional events, and conducts workshops across the country. She and her husband Jeff reside in Minnesota.

Timothy Brown

Timothy Brown did his undergraduate studies at Bowling Green State University and received his master's degree in piano performance from the University of North Texas. His numerous credits as a composer include the first prize at the Aliénor International Harpsichord Competition for his harpsichord solo *Suite Española* (Centaur records). His recent commissions and performances include world premieres by the Chapman University Chamber Orchestra and Concert Choir, the Carter Albrecht Music Foundation, the Rodgers Center for Holocaust Education, and the Daniel Pearl Music Foundation. Timothy Brown is an exclusive composer/clinician for The FJH Music Company Inc.

Martín Cuéllar

Martín Cuéllar enjoys an active and successful career as performer, educator, clinician, and composer. He holds degrees in piano performance from the University of Texas at Austin (DMA, MM) and the Royal Conservatory of Music in Madrid, Spain (performance certificate) where he studied on the music of Enrique Granados at the Marshall Academy of Music in Barcelona (formerly the Granados Academy). As a performer, Dr. Cuéllar has played concerts in the United States, Mexico, Brazil, Spain, Germany, and China. He is also nationally recognized as a composer of pedagogical piano and is published by The FJH Music Company—publisher of not only his pedagogical compositions, but academic editions as well. Dr. Cuéllar serves as associate professor of piano at Emporia State University in Emporia, Kansas.

Lee Evans

Lee Evans, professor of music and former chairperson of the Theatre & Fine Arts Department of Pace University in New York City, graduated from New York City's High School of Music & Art and completed degrees at New York University and Columbia University, receiving his Master of Arts and Doctor of Education from the latter. Professionally, he concertized for ten consecutive seasons under the auspices of Columbia Artists Management, and has performed on some of the world's most prestigious stages, including the White House. He is an acclaimed educator, performer, lecturer, composer, and arranger, and is author of over 90 published music books. Dr. Evans has worked to show it is possible for classical piano teachers with no prior jazz experience to teach jazz concepts with the same skill and discipline as classical music.

FJH2246

ABOUT THE COMPOSERS AND ARRANGERS

Nancy Lau

Nancy Lau (pronounced "Law") has often been told that her music sounds very lyrical and natural. She discovered her love and talent for music early in life. Born with perfect pitch, by age four Nancy was able to play nursery rhymes on the piano by ear. She was soon coming up with her own arrangements of songs and was able to copy any music that she heard. An active composer, arranger, and piano teacher, Nancy studied music composition with Dr. Norman Weston and piano pedagogy with Nakyong Chai at Saddleback College in Orange County, California. In addition to writing for piano, she has composed for solo voice and chamber ensemble, and has written many choral works. Her compositions have won numerous awards. Nancy maintains a full piano studio, where her emphasis is on keeping music enjoyable and exciting. She believes that students must feel nurtured and accepted, and strives to generate in her piano lessons a joyful experience and positive memory.

Edwin McLean

Edwin McLean is a composer living in Chapel Hill, North Carolina. He is a graduate of the Yale School of Music, where he studied with Krzysztof Penderecki and Jacob Druckman. He also holds a master's degree in music theory and a bachelor's degree in piano performance from the University of Colorado. Mr. McLean has authored over 200 publications for The FJH Music Company, ranging from *The FJH Classic Music Dictionary* to original works for pianists from beginner to advanced. His highly-acclaimed works for harpsichord have been performed internationally and are available on the Miami Bach Society recording, *Edwin McLean: Sonatas for 1, 2, and 3 Harpsichords*. His 2011 solo jazz piano album *Don't Say Goodbye* (CD1043) includes many of his advanced works for piano published by FJH. Edwin McLean began his career as a professional arranger. Currently, he is senior editor for The FJH Music Company Inc.

Valerie Roth Roubos

Valerie Roth Roubos earned degrees in music theory, composition, and flute performance from the University of Wyoming. Ms. Roubos maintains a studio in her home in Spokane, Washington, where she teaches flute, piano, and composition. Active as a performer, adjudicator, lecturer, and accompanist, Ms. Roubos has lectured and taught master classes at the Washington State Music Teachers Conference, Holy Names Music Camp, and the Spokane and Tri-Cities chapters of Washington State Music Teachers Association. In 2001, the South Dakota Music Teachers Association selected Ms. Roubos as Composer of the Year, and with MTNA commissioned her to write *An American Portrait: Scenes from the Great Plains*, published by The FJH Music Company Inc. Ms. Roubos was chosen to be the 2004–2005 composer-in-residence at Washington State University. In 2006, WSMTA selected her as Composer of the Year.